T0019426

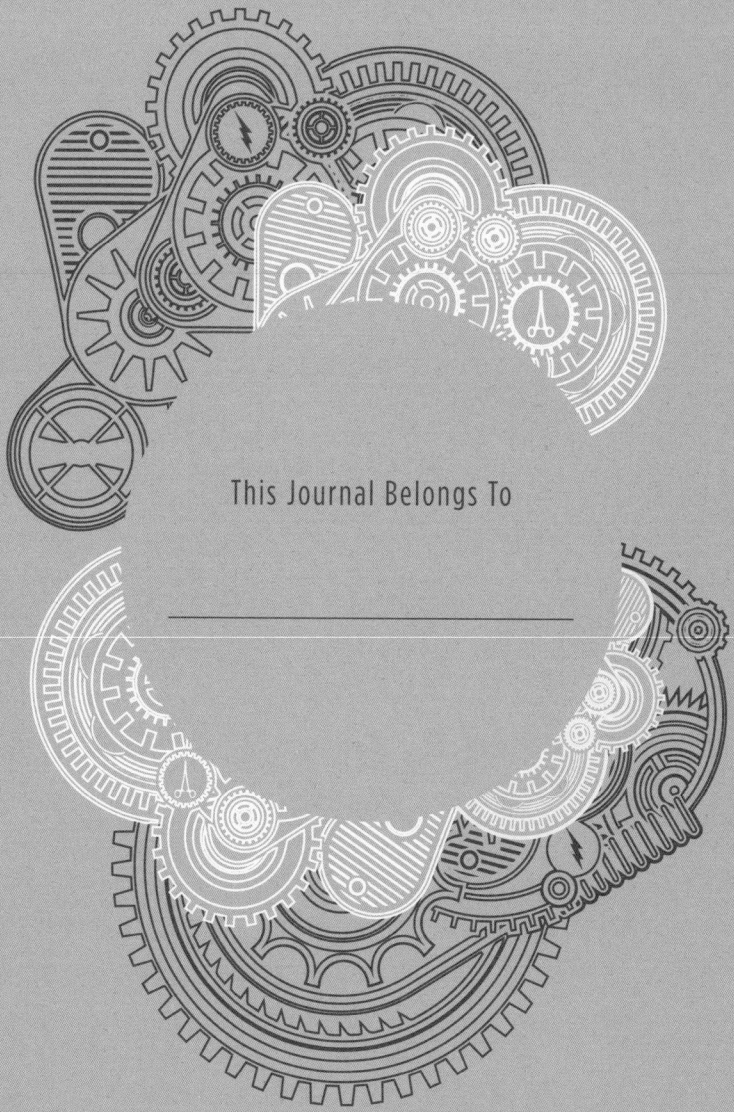

This Journal Belongs To

_____

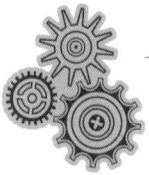

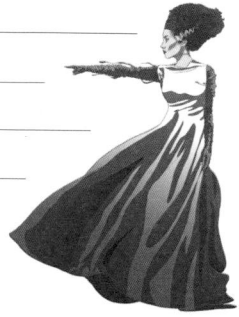

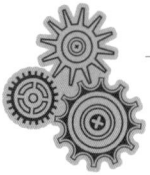

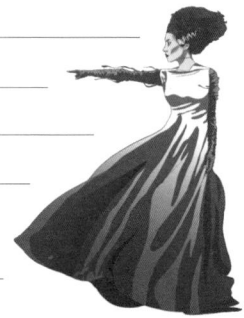

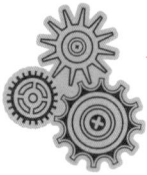

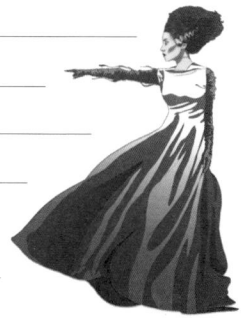

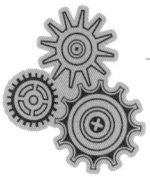

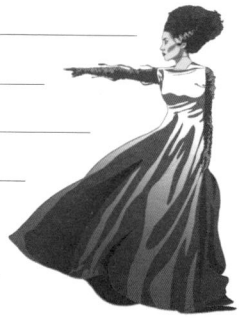

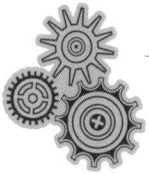

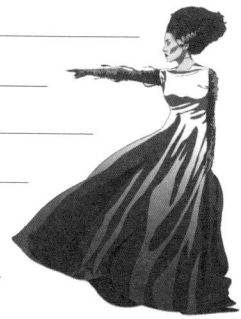

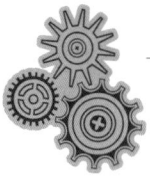

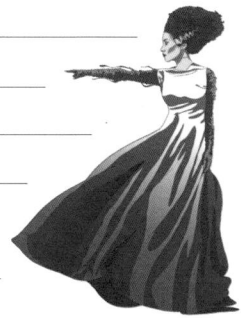

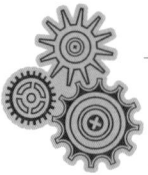

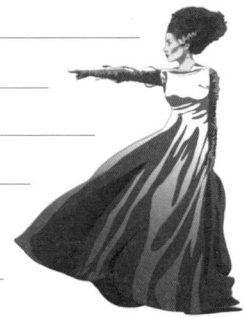

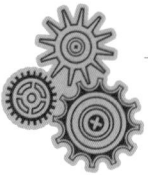

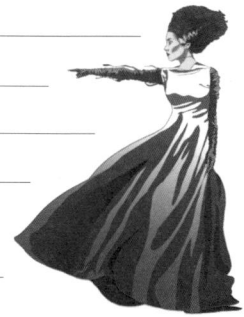

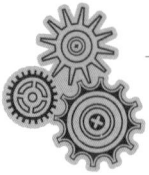

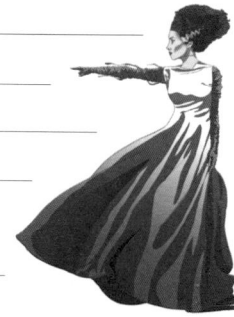

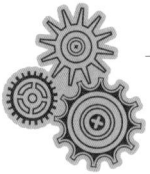

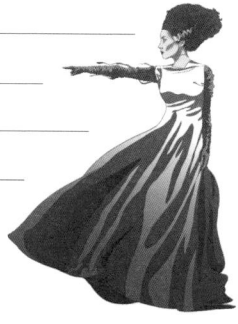

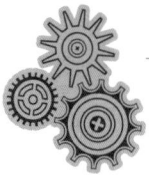

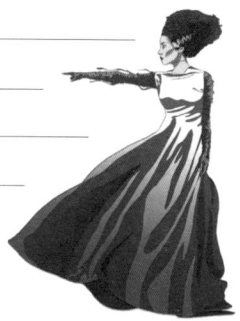

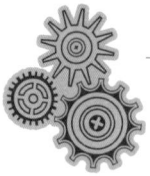

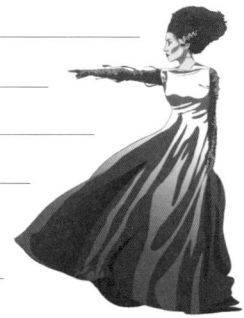

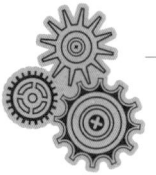

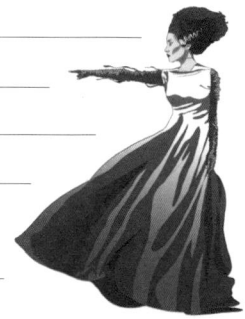

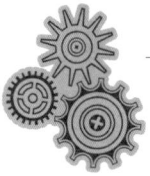

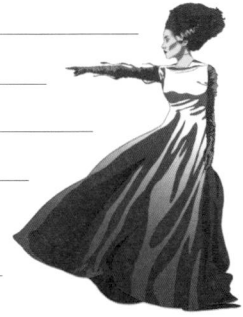

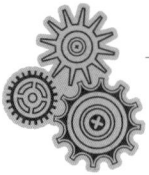

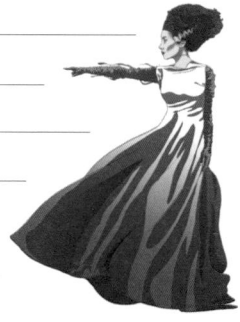

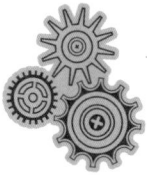

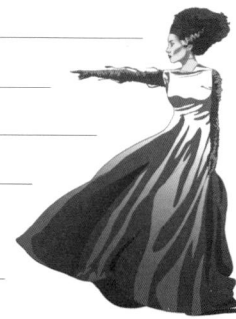

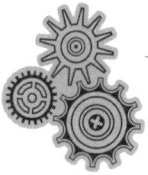

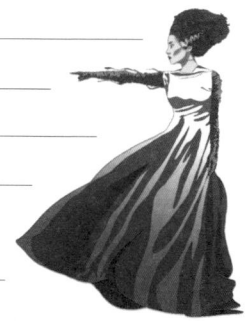

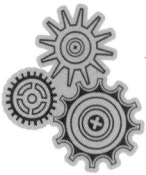

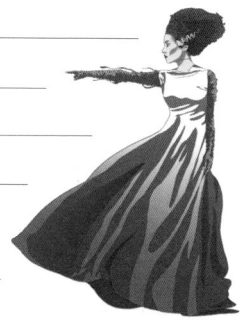

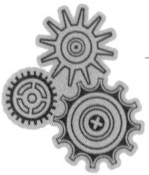

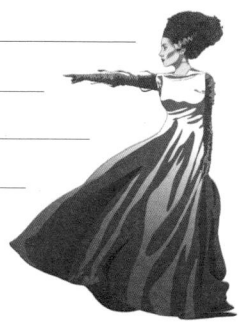

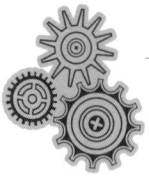

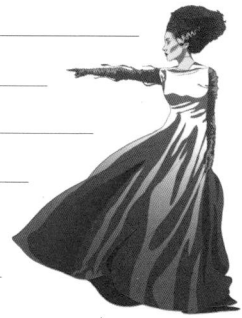

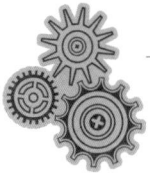

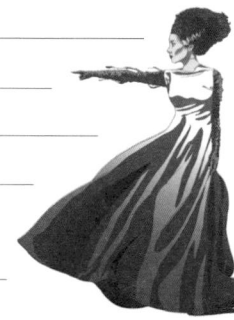

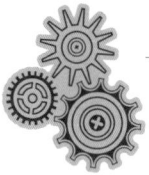

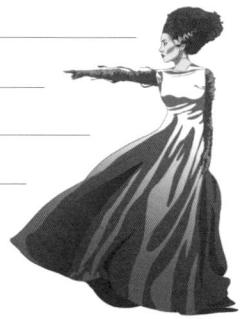

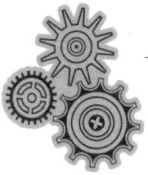

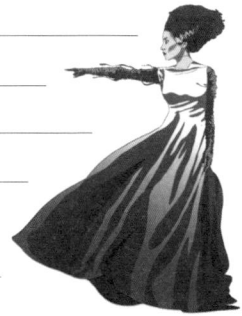

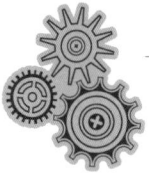

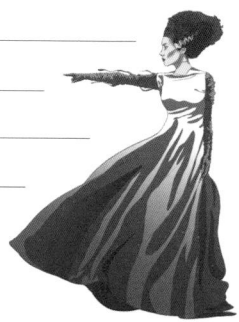

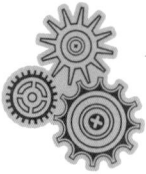

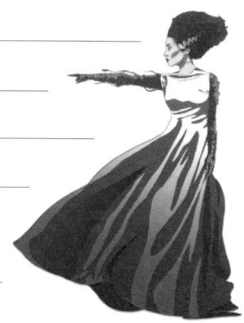

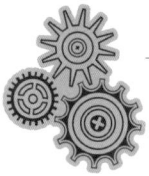

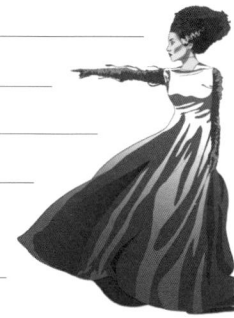

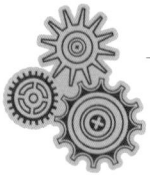

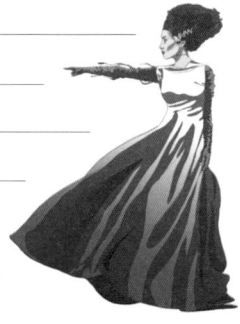

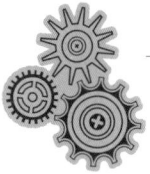

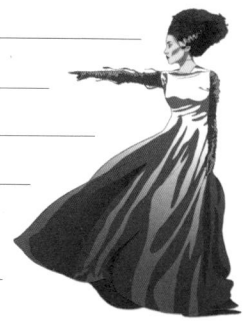

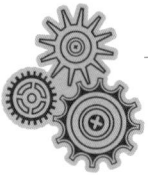

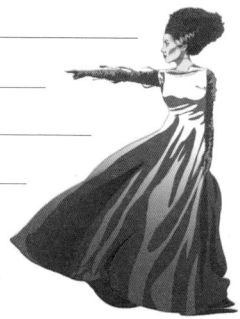

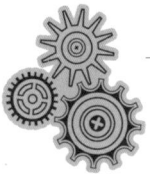

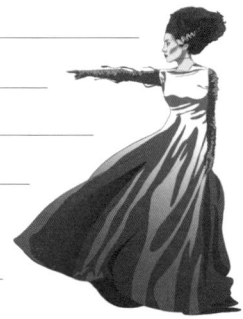

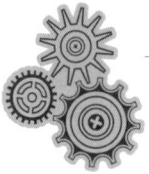

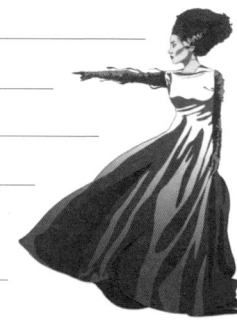

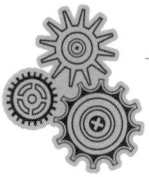

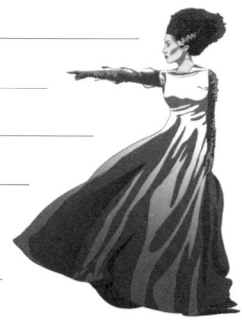

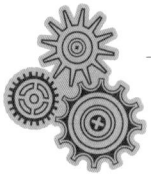

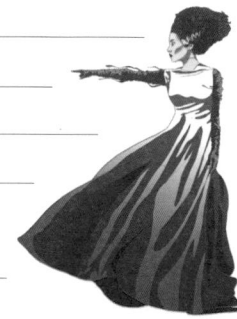

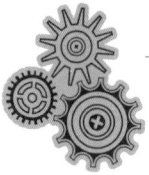

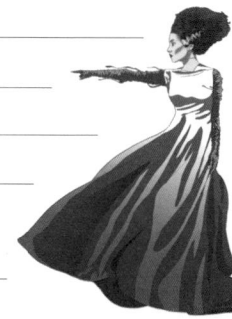

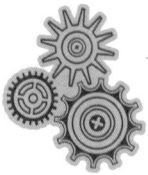

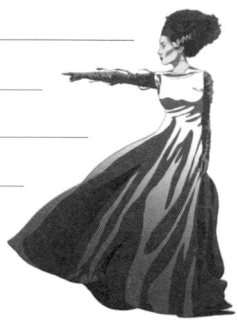

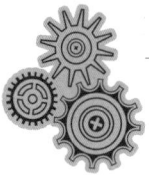

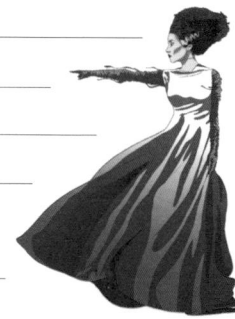

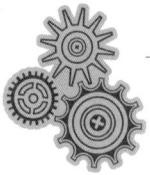

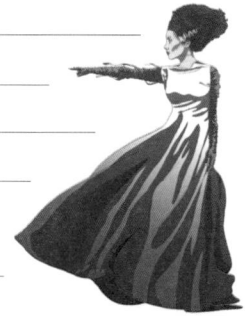

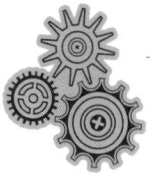

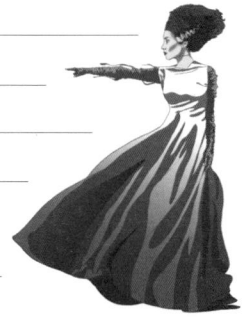

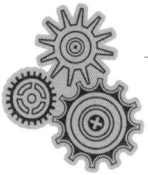

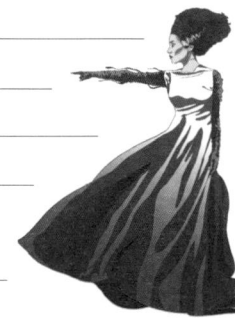

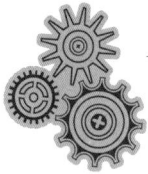

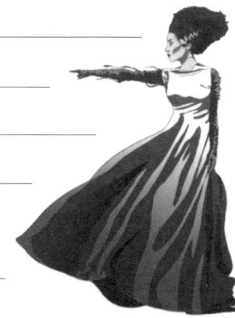

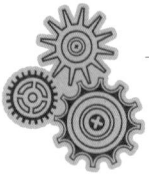

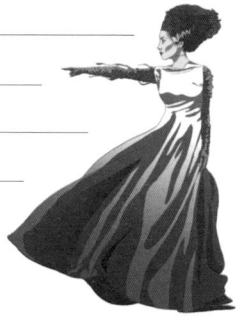

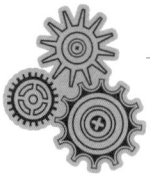

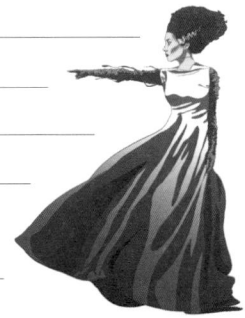

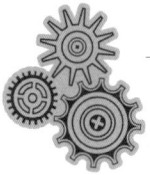

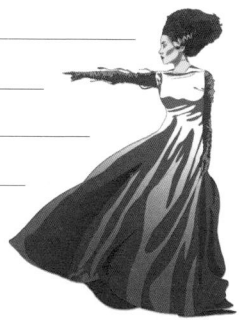

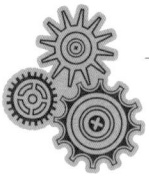

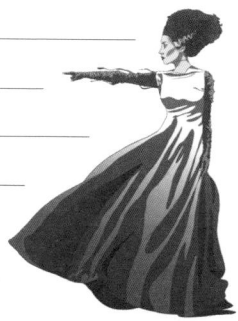

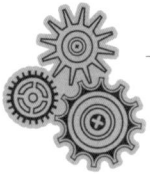

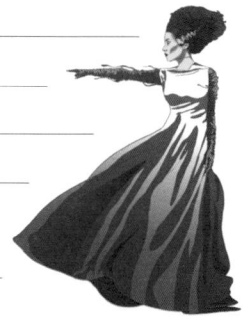

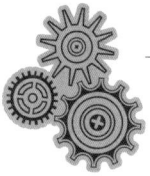

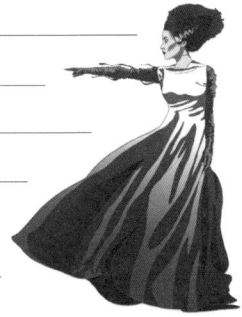

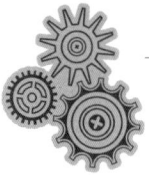

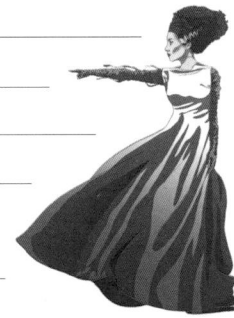

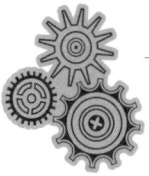

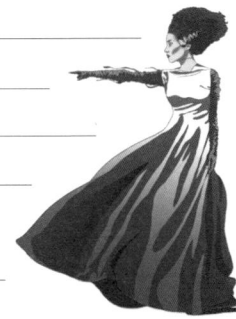

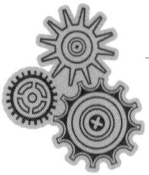

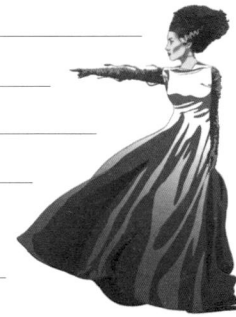

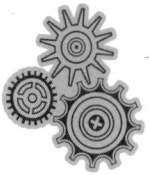

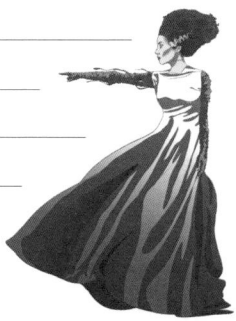

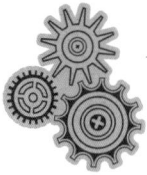

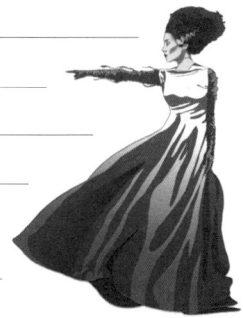

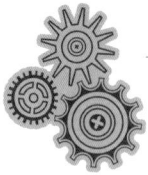

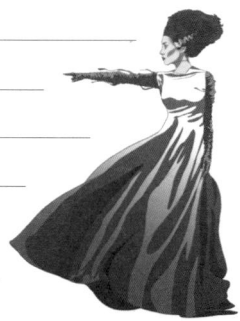

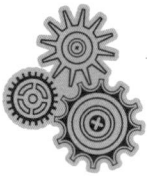

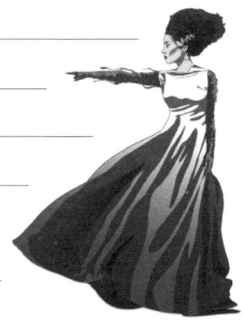

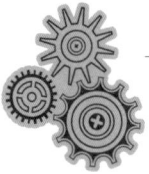

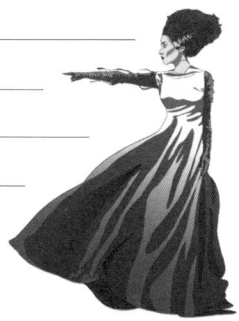

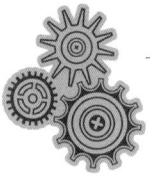

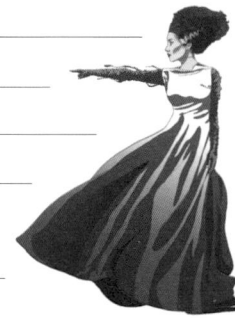

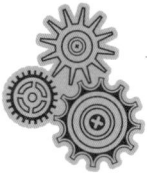

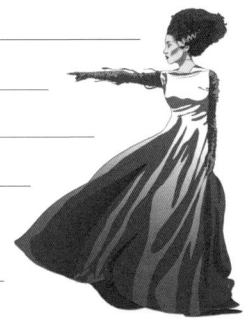

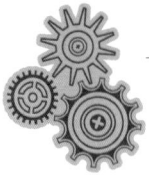

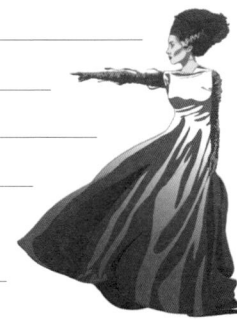

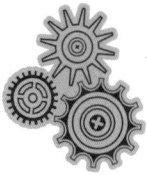

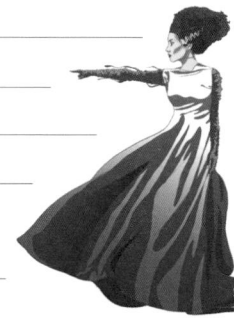

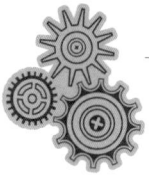

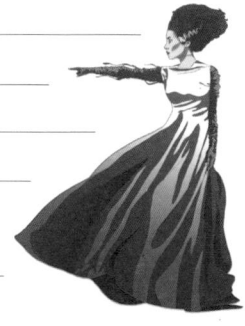

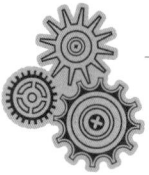

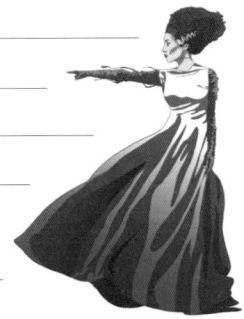

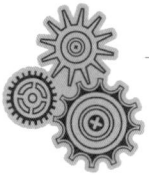

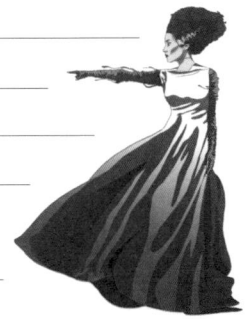

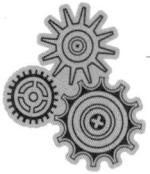

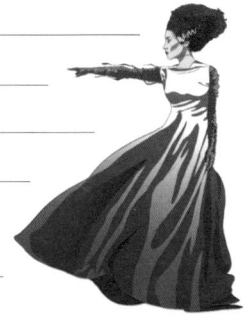

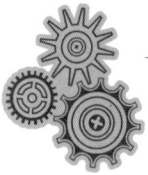

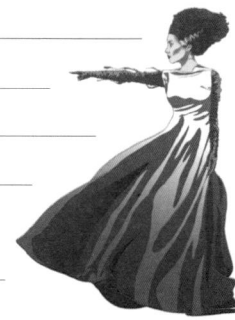

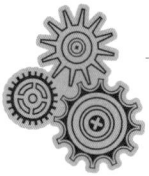

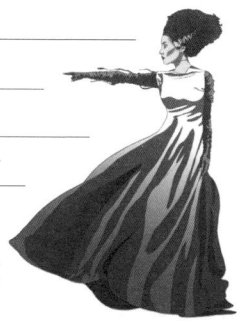

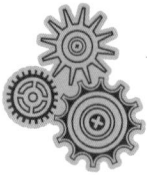

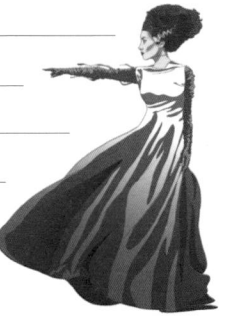

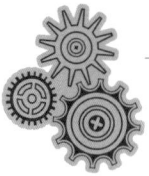

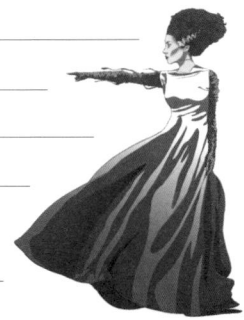

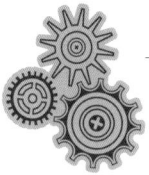

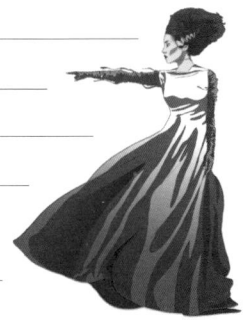

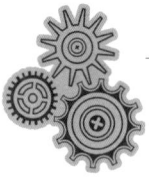

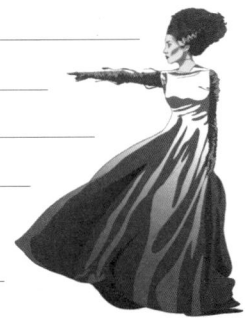

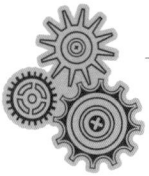

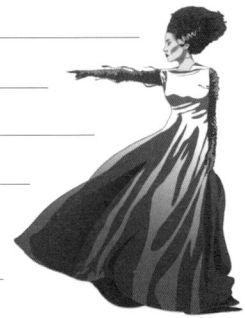

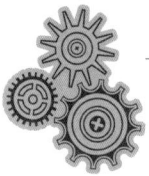

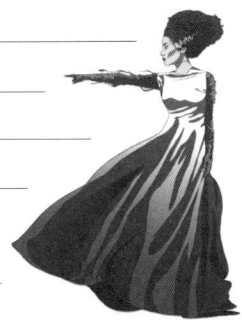

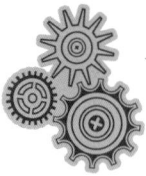

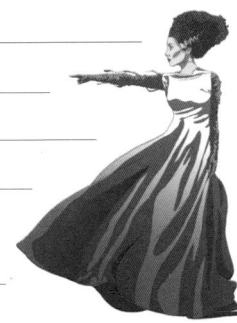

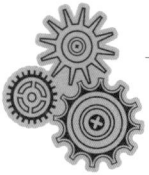

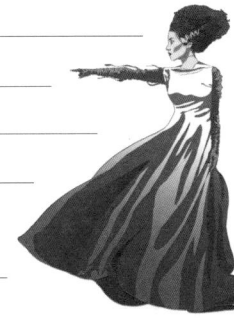

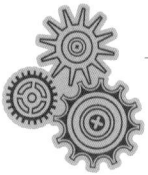

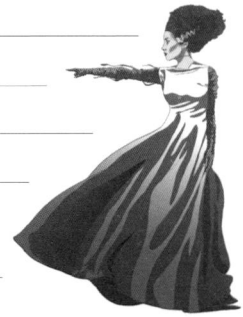

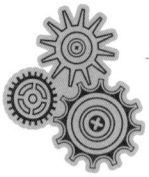

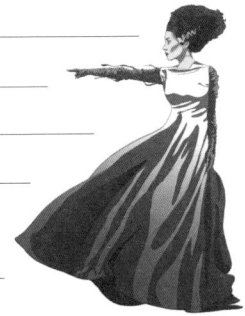

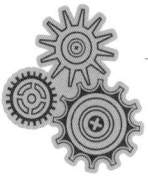

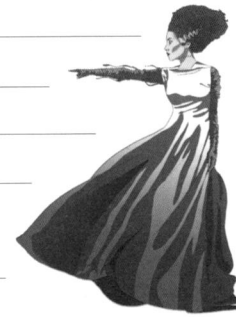

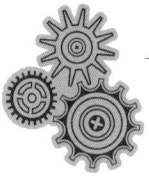

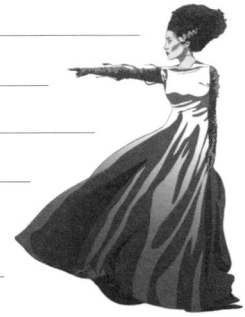

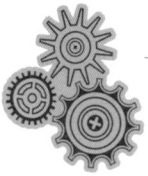

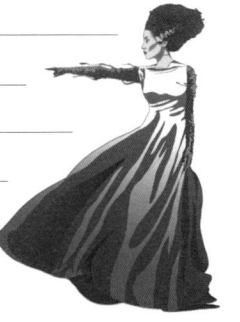

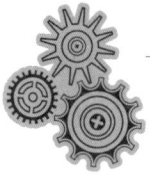

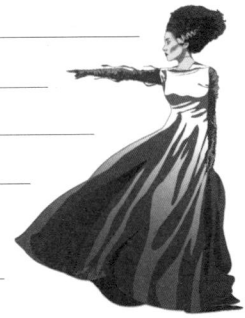

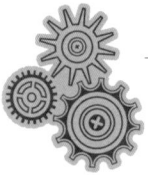

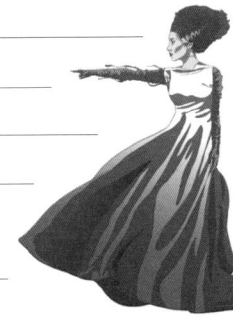

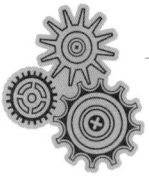

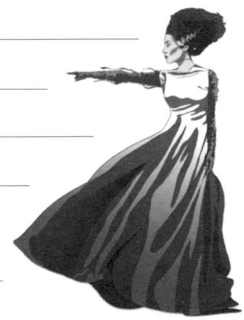

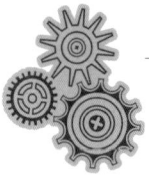

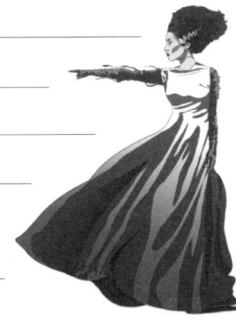

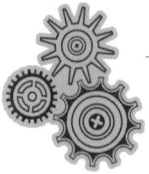

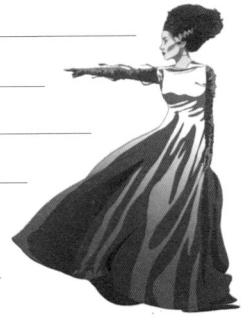

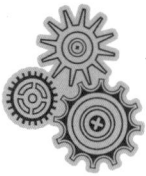

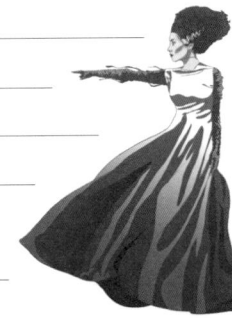

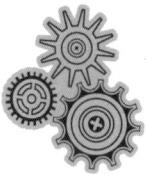

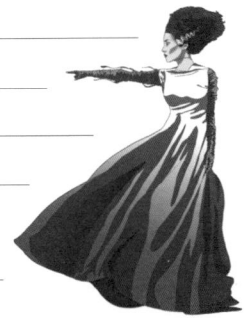

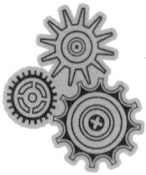

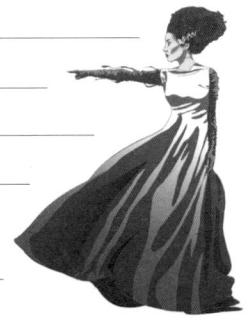

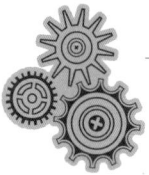

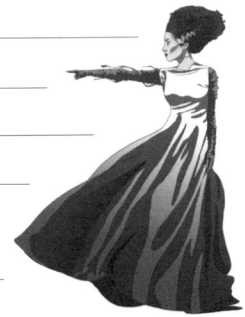

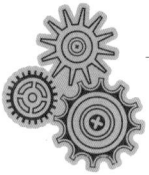

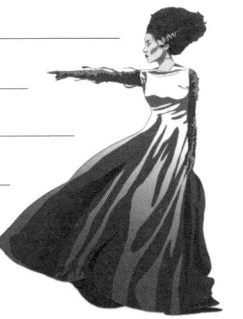

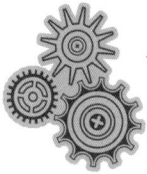

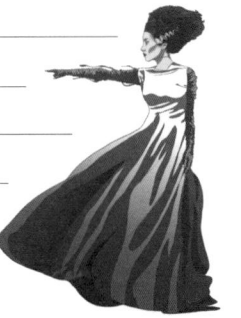

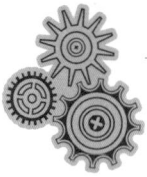

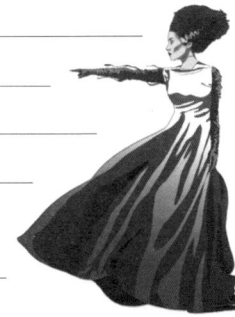

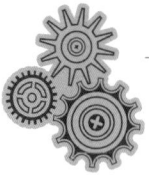

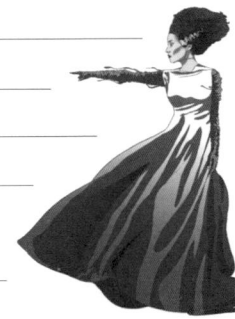

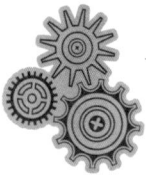

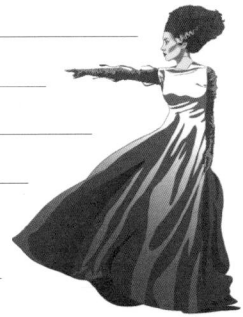

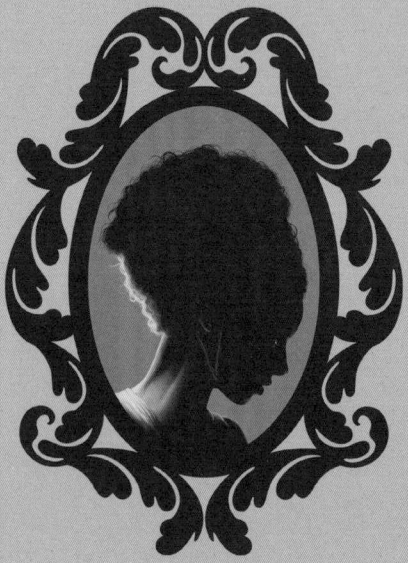

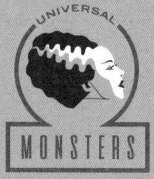

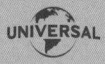

© Universal City Studios LLC.
All Rights Reserved.

INSIGHTS
insighteditions.com

MANUFACTURED IN CHINA
10 9 8 7 6 5 4 3 2 1

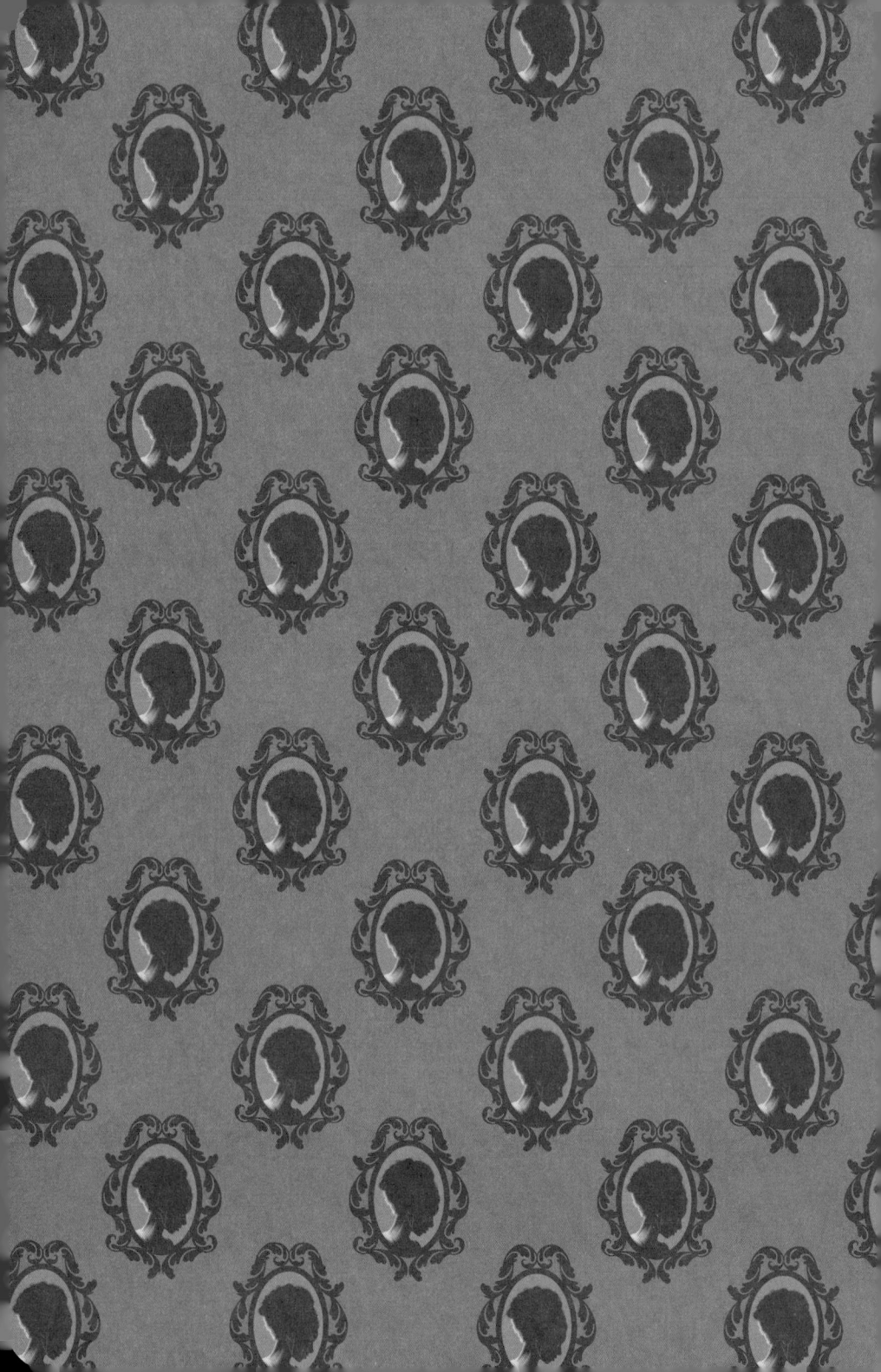